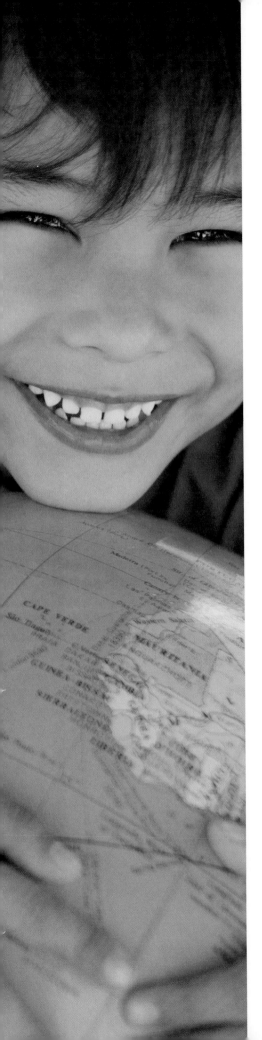

Social Studies Alive!®
Me and My World

Chief Executive Officer
Bert Bower

Chief Operating Officer
Amy Larson

Director of Product Development
Maria Favata

Strategic Product Manager
Nathan Wellborne

Content Developer
Ginger Wu

Senior Strategic Editor
Kim Merlino

Program Editors and Writers
Mikaila Garfinkel
Sally Isaacs
Glenda Stewart
Kelly Stewart
Alex White
Ginger Wu

Production Manager
Jodi Forrest

Operations & Software Manager
Marsha Ifurung

Designer
Sarah Osentowski

Art Direction
Julia Foug

Teachers' Curriculum Institute
PO Box 1327
Rancho Cordova, CA 95741

Customer Service: 800-497-6138
www.teachtci.com

ISBN 978-1-58371-034-0
2 3 4 5 6 7 8 9 10 -WC- 20 19 18 17

Manufactured by Webcrafters, Inc., Madison, WI
United States of America, June 2017, Job 130623

Program Consultant

Vicki LaBoskey, Ph.D.
Professor of Education
Mills College, Oakland, California

Reading Specialist

Barbara Schubert, Ph.D.
Reading Specialist
Saint Mary's College, Moraga, California

Social Studies Content Scholars

Paul A. Barresi, J.D., Ph.D.
Professor of Political Science and
Environmental Law
*Southern New Hampshire University,
Manchester, New Hampshire*

Phillip J. VanFossen, Ph.D.
James F. Ackerman Professor of Social
Studies Education and Associate Director,
Purdue Center for Economic Education
Purdue University, West Lafayette, Indiana

Fred Walk
Lecturer, Department of Geography
Instructional Assistant Professor,
Department of History
Illinois State University, Normal, Illinois

Wyatt Wells, Ph.D.
Professor of History
Auburn Montgomery, Alabama

Literature Consultant

Regina M. Rees, Ph.D.
Assistant Professor
*Beeghly College of Education, Youngstown
State University, Youngstown, Ohio*

Teacher Consultants

Abby Bradski
Teacher
*Walter Hayes Elementary,
Palo Alto, California*

Gina Frazzini
Literary Coach
Gatzert Elementary, Seattle, Washington

Patrick J. Lee
Teacher
Ohlone Elementary, Palo Alto, California

Elana Levine
Teacher
Haisley Elementary, Ann Arbor, Michigan

Paige Martinez
Teacher
Old Orchard School, Campbell, California

Hanan Masri
Teacher
Berkwood Hedge School, Berkeley, California

Mitch Pascal
Social Studies Specialist
Arlington County Schools, Arlington, Virginia

Eileen Perkins
Teacher
Daves Avenue School, Los Gatos, California

Lisa West
Instructional Specialist, Language Arts/
Social Studies
Landis Elementary School, Houston, Texas

English Language Arts & Literacy and *Social Studies Alive!*

Social Studies Alive! is aligned with the Common Core State Standards for English Language Arts & Literacy[1] (CCELA) to ensure that students develop literacy skills through learning social studies. The K–5 CCELA are organized around four college and career readiness strands: reading, writing, speaking and listening, and language.

Key Points from the ELA Common Core	*Social Studies Alive!*
Reading	
Informational and literary texts should be balanced, with at least 50 percent of reading time devoted to expository texts.	*Social Studies Alive!* reflects this balance in the Student Text. Each lesson has several sections of purely informational text that explain the content of that lesson, followed by a Reading Further article that blends literary and informational style text to engage students.
There is a "staircase" of increasing complexity in what students must be able to read as they move throughout the grades.	*Social Studies Alive!* is written with close attention paid to the text complexity, with increasingly sophisticated text as students progress through the grades. However, within each grade's text, there is variation in the complexity to ensure that there is challenging text for all students.
Close reading of text is used to identify main ideas, supporting details, and evidence.	*Social Studies Alive!* Reading Notes in the Interactive Student Notebook require students to answer questions using evidence from the text and require a clear understanding of the main ideas and other details provided in the section.
Writing	
Routine production of writing appropriate for a range of tasks, purposes, and audiences is emphasized.	From the earliest grades, *Social Studies Alive!* students practice three types of writing—writing to persuade, writing to inform or explain, and writing to convey experience. For example, when they record Reading Notes, students enjoy the challenges of writing about a personal experience related to the lesson, creating timelines, and writing song lyrics.
Effective use of evidence is central throughout the writing standards.	*Social Studies Alive!* students are expected to use evidence appropriately to support their analysis, reflections, and research. They are given support in identifying key details, which will serve most effectively as evidence. They also reflect on the role evidence plays in the social sciences and argument in general.

[1]National Governors Association Center for Best Practices, Council of Chief State School Officers. *Common Core State Standards for English Language Arts & Literacy in History/Social Studies, Science, and Technical Subjects.* National Governors Association Center for Best Practices, Council of Chief State School Officers, Washington D.C. Date: 2010.

Key Points from the ELA Common Core	Social Studies Alive!

Speaking and Listening

Participation in rich, structured academic conversations in one-on-one, small-group, and whole class situations is emphasized.	The teaching strategies in *Social Studies Alive!* provide varied grouping techniques, resulting in a balance of paired, small group, and whole class discussions in which students reflect on their experiences and understanding of the activities. These discussions are designed to build clear communication skills that are critical to success in social studies and for college and career readiness.
Contributing accurate, relevant information; responding to and building on what others have said; and making comparisons and contrasts are important skills for productive conversations.	The cooperative tolerant classroom conventions emphasized throughout all of TCI's curricula encourage students to respond to and build on ideas and arguments presented by other students. During discussions, *Social Studies Alive!* guides students to compare and contrast relevant experiences across the four disciplines of social studies.

Language

Students should acquire and use general academic and domain-specific words.	*Social Studies Alive!* has a progression of increasingly sophisticated vocabulary built into it. Key terms are used throughout a lesson or the year without overwhelming students with too many unfamiliar words. Every component of *Social Studies Alive!* makes use of the vocabulary and includes activities to help solidify comprehension.
Skills to determine or clarify the meaning of unknown words or phrases are essential.	*Social Studies Alive!* vocabulary terms are previewed at the beginning of the lesson and students complete vocabulary development assignments, such as a Word Parts Log, that trains students to parse words to infer meaning.
Students should demonstrate command of standard English, including grammar, punctuation, and spelling.	Throughout all components of *Social Studies Alive!*, students are expected to demonstrate command of the conventions of written and spoken English. An Editing and Proofreading Checklist is included to help students write with minimal errors.

Considerate Text

Social Studies Alive! is both engaging and helps students read text that is more complex and at a higher level. That's because our authors wrote it as a "considerate text," which is another way of saying that it makes readers want to read it. Here are some ways this book is considerate for all levels of readers.

Short sections, each with an informative title, help beginning readers to understand and remember the lesson's most important points.

5. Solving Problems in Class

Our class solves problems, too.

Some of us want to make robots.

Some want to put on a play.

What can we do?

Sentences always start on a new line, and each section ends at the bottom of a page.

Thoughtfully-selected images help show the main idea and support beginning readers.

6. Voting

We can **vote** on what to do.

I raise my hand for my choice.

The most votes wins.

We will put on a play!

Important new social studies words are in bold blue type. These words are defined in the context of the section and in the illustrated glossary.

Each lesson is carefully constructed so that each section builds on the previous one.

The Four Core Disciplines of Social Studies

Each of the four core disciplines identified by the National Council for the Social Studies in its C3 Framework[2] has a unique set of ideas, tools, and ways of thinking. Each lesson of *Social Studies Alive!* is aligned to one or more of these disciplines.

 Civics

Important ideas of civics are based on understanding government at various levels, the political system, rules and laws, civic engagement, and democratic principles.

 Economics

The idea of "resources" as including human, physical, and natural resources is essential for understanding the economic decisions people, businesses, and governments make in local, national, and global markets.

[2]National Council for the Social Studies (NCSS), *The College, Career, and Civic Life (C3) Framework for Social Studies State Standards: Guidance for Enhancing the Rigor of K–12 Civics, Economics, Geography, and History* (Silver Spring, MD: NCSS, 2013).

Geography

Using maps and other representations of Earth, understanding the relationship between culture and the environment, analyzing how human populations change, and learning that some environmental changes occur on a global scale are all essential aspects of geography.

History

Reasoning about chronological patterns, explaining how people's perspectives can change, working with historical sources, identifying causes and effects, and developing claims from evidence are some of the skills students develop as they study history.

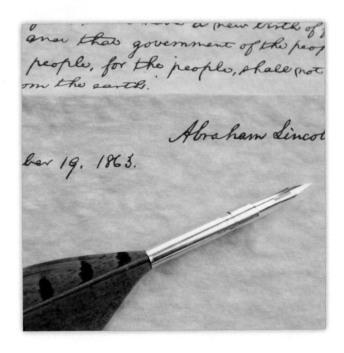

Look for the discipline icons at the beginning of each lesson and Reading Further.

How to Use this Program

Welcome to *Social Studies Alive! Me and My World,* where students learn the basics of citizenship, economics, geography, and history in the context of learning about themselves, their neighborhood, and the world.

1 The teacher begins each lesson with a **Presentation** that previews the lesson and facilitates one or more minds-on or hands-on activities.

2 Classroom Presentations are the heart of *Social Studies Alive!* First, a visual lesson preview engages students and taps their prior knowledge. Next, a hands-on **activity** connects to English Language Arts literacy by using some of the tools of social studies inquiry: asking questions, identifying helpful sources for answering questions, and connecting facts with questions.

3a In the online **Student Subscription,** students expand their knowledge through reading the Student Text and processing what they have learned in the **Interactive Student Notebook.** Students can also play a game-like **Reading Challenge** activity.

3b Alternatively, students can read from the **Student Edition** and complete a consumable Interactive Student Notebook.

4 The lesson ends with students demonstrating their knowledge of the core ideas and essential social studies skills of the lesson through a variety of paper and online **assessments.**

How to Read the Table of Contents

The table of contents is your guide to *Social Studies Alive! Me and My World*. It lists all the lessons in your text.

The **lesson title** is also the lesson's **essential question**.

Every lesson emphasizes one or more of the four **core disciplines** of social studies: Civics, Economics, Geography, and History.

1 Who Am I? 2

I am special.
I can do many things.

Reading Further: The Story of
Our Flag 8

A **summary** of the lesson tells you what you will read about and discover.

Every lesson includes a **Reading Further**—a fun, high-interest article that promotes literacy and helps you engage with the content even further.

Contents

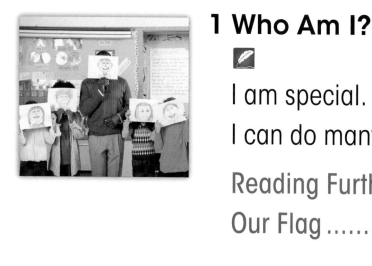

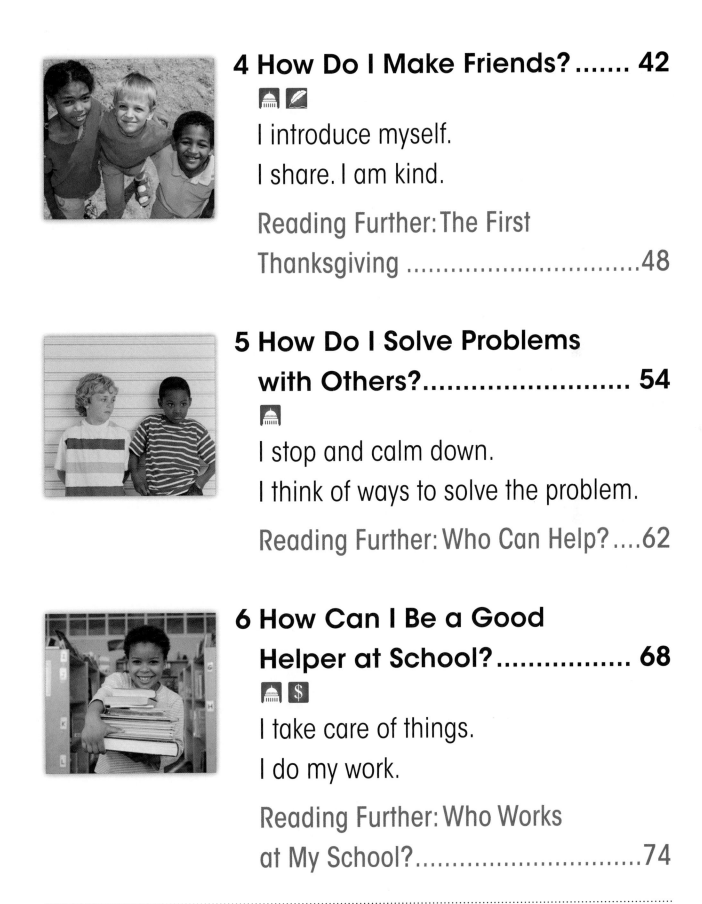

I Can Learn About My World 156

I can learn about my family.

I can learn about my neighborhood.

I can learn about my country.

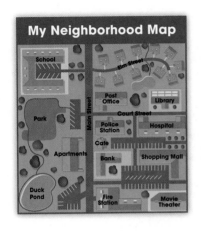

Maps

Primary Sources

You will learn that a primary source of an event is an object created by someone who was there. See for yourself what you can learn about history from old photos.

penny 1¢

dime 10¢

one dollar 100¢

Our Jobs

nickel 5¢

quarter 25¢

half dollar 50¢

October 2016

Sunday Sun.	Monday Mon.	Tuesday Tues.				rday
1	2	3	4	5		
8	9	10	11	12		

Who Am I?

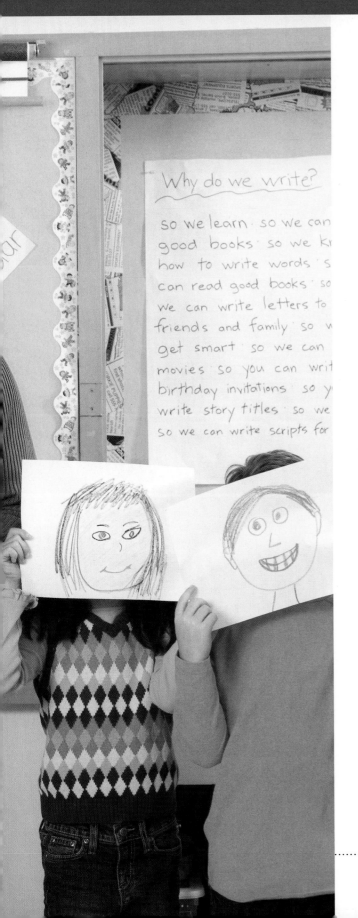

How am I special?

No one looks like me.

No one talks like me.

My Words

feelings

special

History

1. Being Special

I am **special**.

No one looks the way I look.

No one likes all the things I like.

There is only one me.

2. Caring

I care about my family.

To show I care, I give them hugs.

I care about my friends, too.

We help each other out.

3. Feelings

I have many **feelings**.

I can feel happy. I smile.

I can feel angry or sad, too.

Sometimes I am surprised.

4. Doing Many Things

I can do many things.

At school, I draw and sing.

I play sports with friends.

At home, I talk to my family.

The Story of Our Flag

George Washington lived long ago.

He is the father of our country.

He was the first U.S. president.

He led our country.

Betsy Ross sewed for a living.

She was asked to sew

our country's first flag.

She felt proud to do it.

She sewed 13 white stars on blue.

She added 13 red and white stripes.

She worked hard to sew the flag.

It is a symbol of our country.

We say the Pledge of Allegiance.

We recite it to the flag.

But our flag today is different.

What changes do you see?

What Is a Family?

I live with my family.

We care for each other.

We do things together.

My Words

family

tradition

History

1. My Family

I am part of a **family**.

I live with people in my family.

We spend time together.

We all love each other.

2. Caring

Families take care of each other.

Adults take care of children.

Sometimes brothers and sisters
help take care of each other, too.

3. Doing Things Together

Families do things together.

We go for walks outside.

Sometimes we play board games.

What else do families do together?

4. Traditions

Families have **traditions**.

A tradition is something that a family has done for many years. Many holidays have traditions.

5. A Birthday Tradition

Families celebrate birthdays.

Some fill a piñata with treats.

Someone breaks it open.

The treats fall to the ground.

6. A Fall Tradition

Some families eat mooncakes.

The cakes are filled with lotus.

They are eaten for a fall festival.

They celebrate food and family.

7. Thanksgiving Traditions

Many families have

Thanksgiving traditions.

They may eat turkey and pie.

They say "thank you."

8. Valentine's Day Traditions

Schools have traditions, too.

We celebrate Valentine's Day.

I give a card to each classmate.

This shows I care about others.

Our Country's Birthday

Look at a calendar.

Find your birthday.

Our country has a birthday, too.

It is on the Fourth of July.

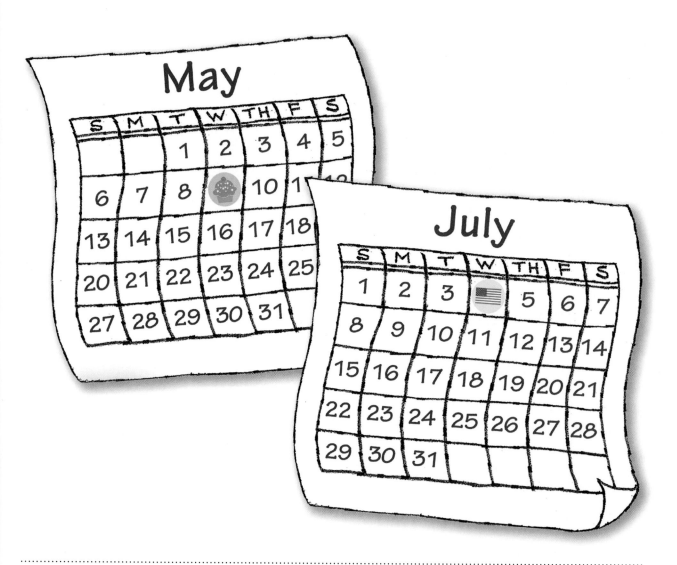

Long ago, America was

ruled by another country.

This country was Great Britain.

The king was in charge.

Life was different then.

People made their own clothes.

They grew much of their own food.

Children played marbles.

People had to follow British rules.

Many were unhappy.

They wanted to set their own rules.

They wanted their own leaders.

Thomas Jefferson was a leader.

He wrote a paper.

It said why America should be free.

This was more than 200 years ago.

Then he and others signed it.

This was on July 4, 1776.

People in America were free.

Our country was born on this day.

Today, we celebrate America's birthday on July 4th.

Some families have a picnic.

Others might watch fireworks.

We all show pride for

our country on this day.

We wear red, white, and blue.

We wave the American flag.

How Do I Get Along with Others?

I try to get along.

I am a good listener.

I take turns.

My Words

get along

 Civics

1. Talking

I talk when it is my turn.

I do not talk while others talk.

In class, I raise my hand.

Then I can answer questions.

2. Listening

I listen while others talk.

How am I a good listener?

I face the person talking to me.

I only talk when they are done.

3. Taking Turns

I take turns with others.

Sometimes, I wait in line.

I get to go, and then you go.

This helps us **get along**.

4. Making Choices

I make good choices.

I help a friend who is hurt.

If I make a mess, I clean it up.

What other choices do I make?

Civics

Rules Help Us

Rules help us get along.

Games have rules.

When I follow the rules,

it is fun for all of us.

There are rules in class, too.

I raise my hand to speak.

I am a good listener.

I am kind to others.

My family teaches

me rules at home.

I clean up after myself.

I do not run or shout inside.

Rules also keep us safe.

I cross the street with an adult.

We wait until the light is green.

I look both ways before I go.

Adults teach me rules.

My teacher makes

sure I follow them.

I learn how to act at school.

It is important to follow rules.

When I don't,

others might feel left out.

Or I might get hurt.

How Do I Make Friends?

How do I make friends?

I talk to others.

I play with them, too.

My Words

introduce

 Civics

1. Introducing Myself

I **introduce** myself to others.

First, I tell them my name.

Then, they tell me theirs.

I smile and am polite.

2. Asking Friends to Play

I ask a friend to play

blocks with me.

She may say "yes."

She may kindly say "no."

3. Sharing

I share with others at school.

We share toys, books,

tape, and markers.

What else can we share?

4. Being Kind

I am kind to others.

I treat everyone the same.

At school, I help my classmates.

This makes me a good friend.

The First Thanksgiving

Almost 400 years ago,

the Pilgrims came to America.

They sailed from England.

They came to find a new home.

When they came, it was winter.

The Pilgrims worked hard.

They built wood houses.

They cleared land to grow food.

New friends helped the Pilgrims.

One was named Squanto.

He was an American Indian

of the Wampanoag tribe.

It was the tribe's way to be

polite and kind to strangers.

Squanto helped the Pilgrims.

He taught them to grow corn.

The Pilgrims were thankful.

They celebrated with a feast.

Wampanoag people came.

They shared food and gave thanks.

We remember this event.

It is called Thanksgiving.

We share food with family.

We say why we are thankful.

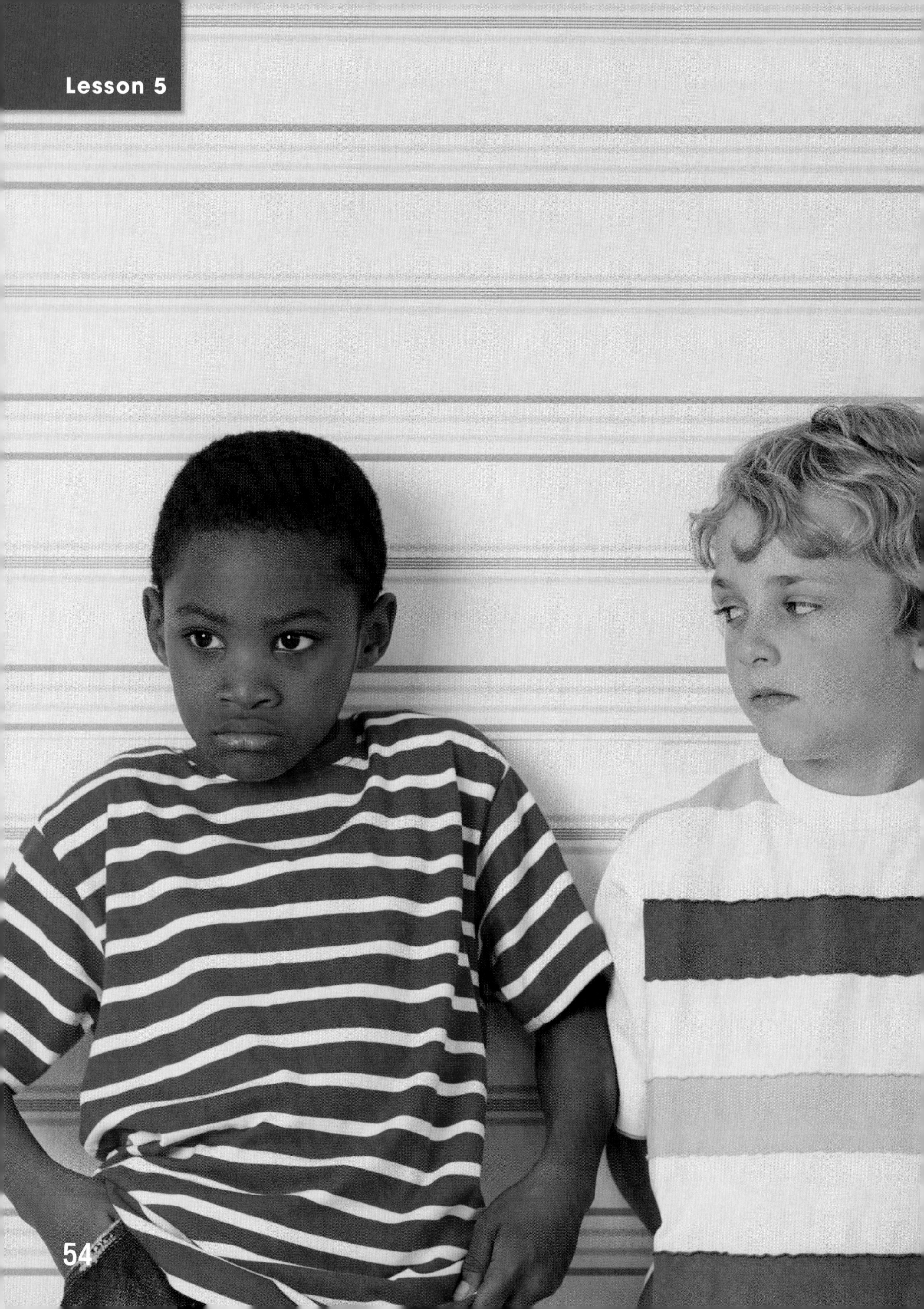

How Do I Solve Problems with Others?

We have a problem.

How can we fix it?

We solve it together.

My Words

calm down

problem

solve

vote

Civics

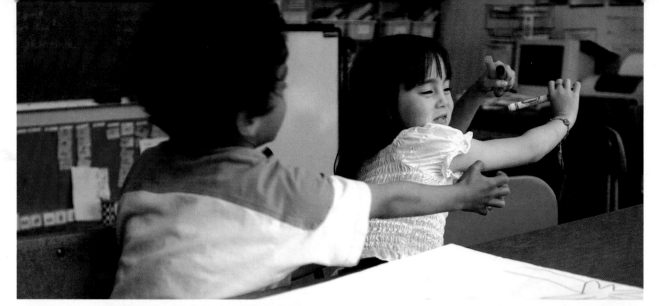

1. Calming Down

My friend and I have a **problem**.

We both want the same marker.

I feel upset. What can we do?

First, I stop and **calm down**.

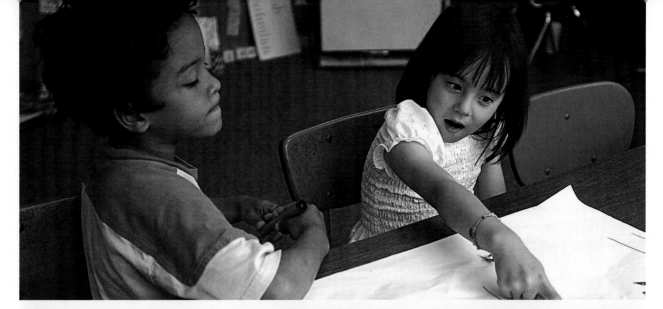

2. Talking and Listening

Next, we talk and listen.

I say why my feelings are hurt.

Then my friend does the same.

We listen to each other.

3. Solving Problems

Now we think of ways

to **solve** the problem.

I share my ideas.

Then you share yours.

4. Trying a Plan

We agree on a plan.

Then we try it.

If our plan doesn't work,

we can try another one.

5. Solving Problems in Class

Our class solves problems, too.

Some of us want to make robots.

Some want to put on a play.

What can we do?

6. Voting

We can **vote** on what to do.

I raise my hand for my choice.

The most votes wins.

We will put on a play!

Who Can Help?

Solving problems can be hard.

Sometimes I get stuck.

I can ask an adult for help.

We can solve it together.

My family and I go to the park.

Suddenly, I lose my parents.

I ask a police officer for help.

He keeps me safe and finds them.

I wake up sick.

My throat feels sore.

I go to the doctor.

She helps me feel better.

I am on the bus to school.

I forgot my backpack!

I let the bus driver know.

He helps me get my backpack.

I have a problem at school.

Today, we are working in pairs.

But I do not have a partner.

Who can I ask for help?

I tell my teacher the problem.

She helps me solve it.

She finds a pair of students.

We work in a group of three.

How Can I Be a Good Helper at School?

We can help at school.

Then it is a better place.

How can I help?

My Words

directions

Civics

1. Taking Care of Things

I help take care of things.

I treat objects with care

so they will last longer.

I feed the class pet.

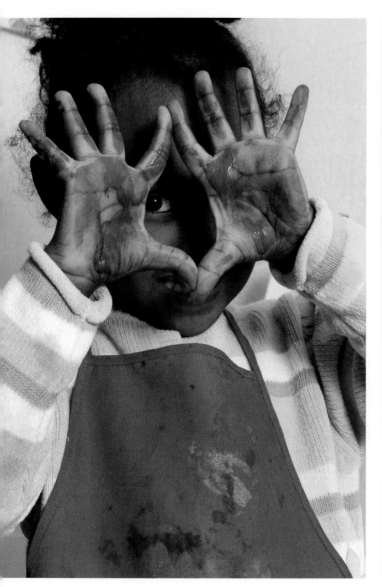
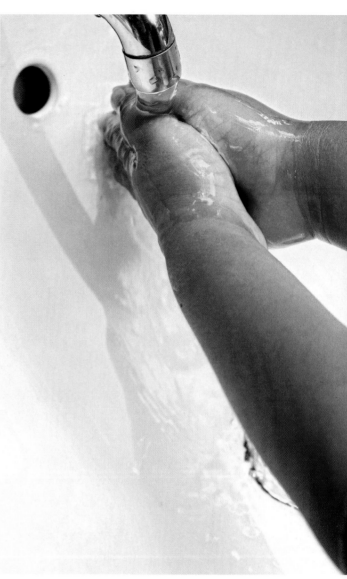

2. Cleaning Up

I help keep my school clean.

After I use something,

I put it away. I wash up.

I throw away my trash.

3. Following Directions

I listen to my teacher and
follow **directions**.

Then I know what to do.

I obey the school rules.

4. Doing My Work

I do my work so I can learn.

I ask questions.

I finish my work on time.

I work well with others.

Who Works at My School?

Many people work at a school.

Who works at my school?

How do they help me?

Let's find out!

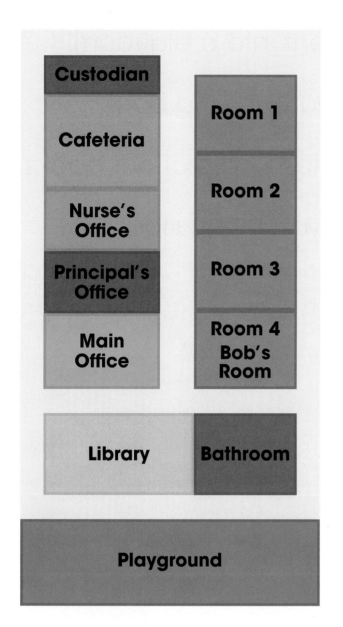

Bob is our class's pet rabbit.

One day, we found his door open.

He was not in the classroom.

Where did Bob go?

First, Bob went into a big room.

He saw a woman and books.

She said, "I take care of our books.

Can I help you find a story?"

Librarian

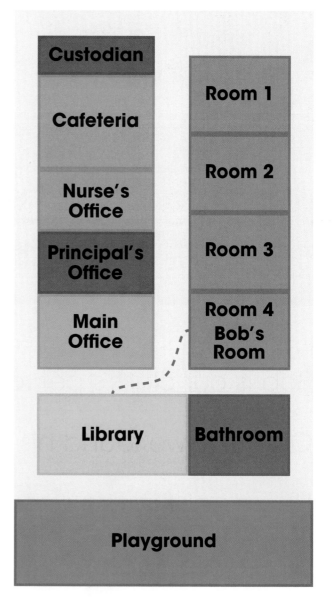

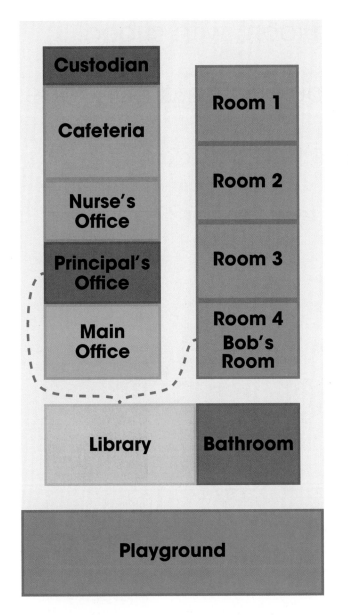

Principal

Bob left and went into an office.

The door's sign began with *P*.

A man said, "I'm a school leader.

Can I help solve a problem?"

Bob went into a room with a bed.

A woman was putting on a bandage.

She said, "I treat pains.

Can I help you feel better?"

School Nurse

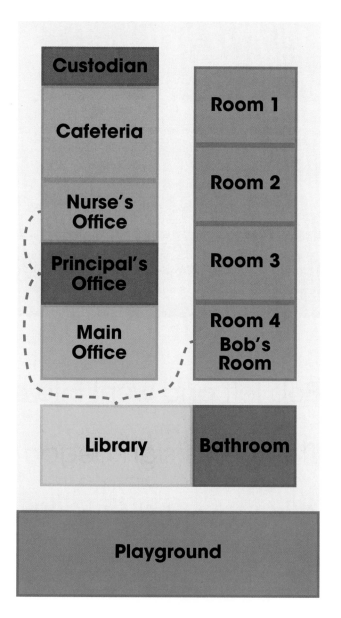

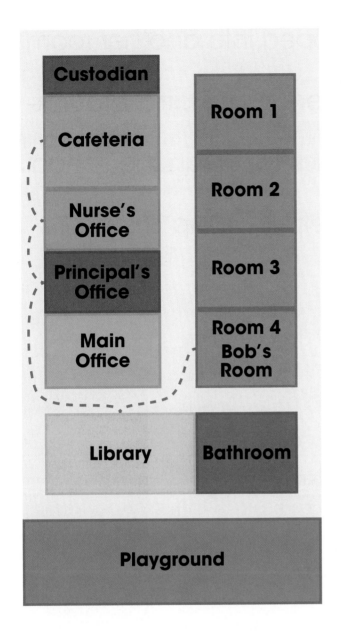

School Cook

Then Bob smelled food.

This room had pots and pans.

A man said, "I cook hot lunches.

Can I get you lunch to eat?"

Bob hopped into another room.

There were mops and brooms.

A man said, "I clean the school.

Can I help mop up a spill?"

Custodian

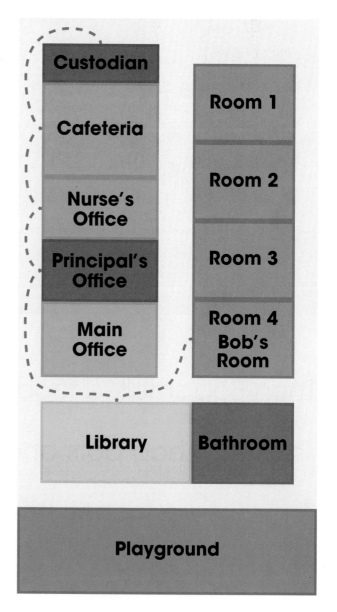

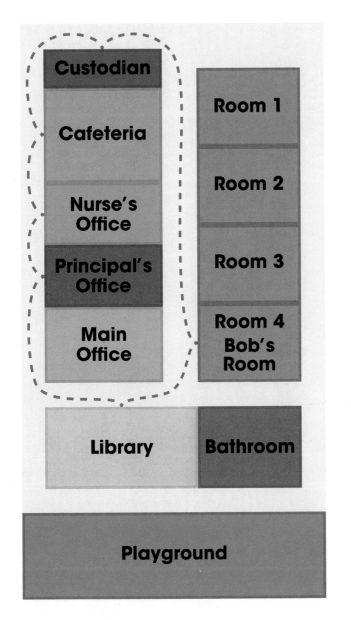

Teacher

Finally, Bob found his classroom.

A woman picked him up.

She said, "Were you lost, Bob?

I can teach you to read a map."

What Is in My Neighborhood?

People live and work in my neighborhood. I live here, too.

My Words

map

neighbor

neighborhood

Geography

1. Buildings Where I Live

My **neighborhood** has buildings.

There are many homes.

I live in an apartment.

My friend lives in a house.

There are stores and schools, too.

There is a sign over the bank door.

People sit in front of the café.

Tables are under the umbrellas.

2. Outdoors Where I Live

A neighborhood has outdoor areas.

My dad and I sit near the pond.

I slide behind friends at the park.

My friends run along the paths.

There are objects outdoors.

A sign says, "Stop."

Another means "left turn."

Across the road is a fountain.

Map Key

land
water
road

3. Neighborhood Maps

A **map** shows what a place

looks like from above.

What does the map key show?

Land is green. Water is blue.

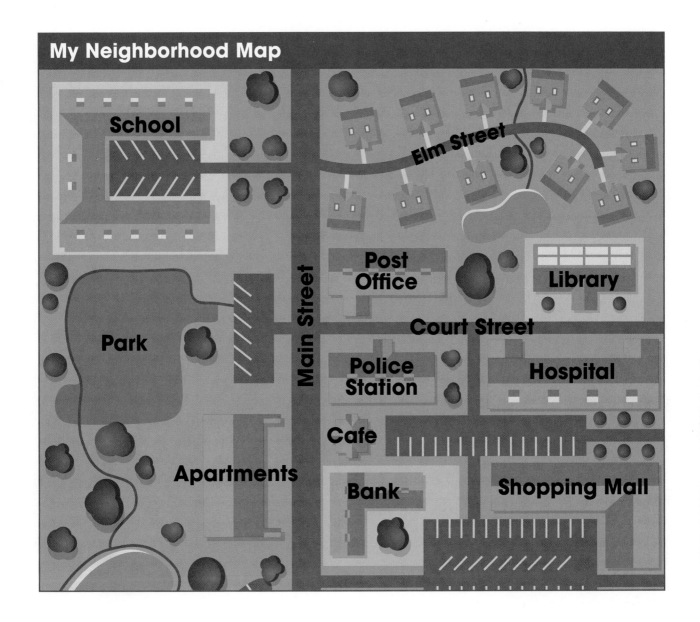

My Neighborhood Map

School

Elm Street

Post Office

Library

Main Street

Court Street

Park

Police Station

Hospital

Cafe

Apartments

Bank

Shopping Mall

I can use a map to find things.

The school is near the park.

The pond is far from the library.

The cafe is next to the bank.

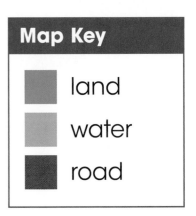

Map Key

land

water

road

4. My Neighbors

My neighborhood has people.

The people who live and work

nearby are my **neighbors**.

My neighbors are all different.

Some neighbors are old and tall.

Some are young and small.

I am part of my neighborhood!

Who are your neighbors?

History

How Can We Improve Our Neighborhood?

In the past, black people could not do things with white people. They went to different schools. They ate at different cafés.

They had to drink at their

own water fountains.

Those were the laws.

Do they seem fair?

Dr. Martin Luther King Jr. said
the laws were not fair.
He wanted all people to be
treated the same.

Dr. King fought for fair laws.

But he did it with peace.

He spoke strong words.

He made people think and feel.

Many people walked to show

they believed in Dr. King.

Our leaders listened.

They worked to change the laws.

Now, people can

do things together.

Dr. King was brave.

Each January, we honor him.

Other men and women have worked to make change.

Harriet Tubman helped slaves.

Daniel Boone explored places.

You can learn about them.

Who will you study?

What questions can you ask?

What information can you find?

Where Am I in the World?

The world is a big place.

Where do I live?

I can find it on a globe.

My Words

city

country

state

world

Geography

1. Living in a City

I live with my family in a **city**.

Here, there are tall buildings.

I see many trees and a lake.

What else is in our city?

In the summer, it is warm.

I have picnics by the lake.

In the winter, it snows a lot.

My family and I go sledding.

2. Living in a State

My city is in a **state**.

Some parts have mountains.

There are many trees,

and some are made into paper.

There are many things to do.

I can go to a museum,

and I can go camping.

Sometimes, I go to the movies.

The United States

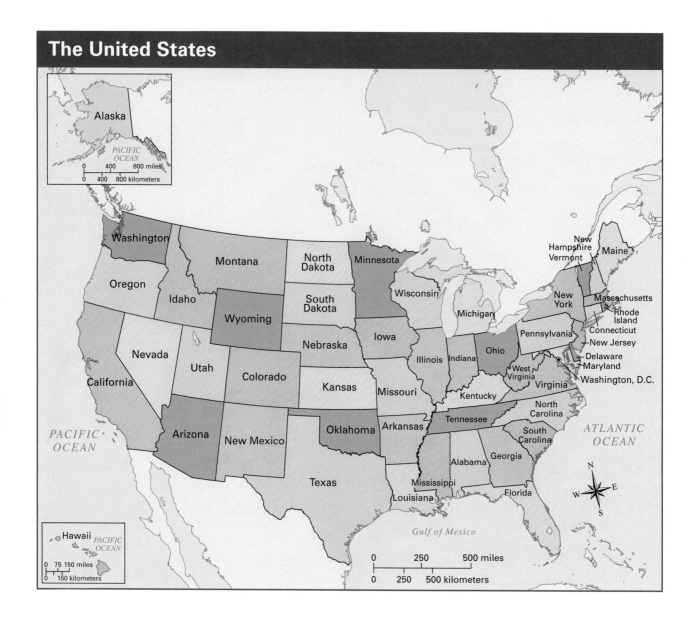

3. Living in a Country

I live in the United States.

It is a **country**. Look at this map.

The states are in different colors.

Find your state. What color is it?

4. Living in the World

I live in the **world**.

This is a picture of the world.

The blue parts show water.

What do the other colors show?

Civics

Symbols of Our Country

Each state has its own flag.

The flag is a symbol.

It stands for the people

and leaders who live there.

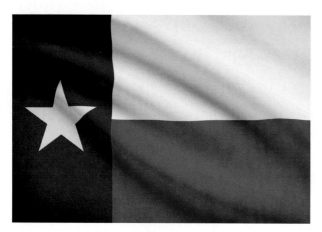

Texas

California

New Hampshire

Washington

Our country has a flag, too.

It waves red, white, and blue.

We are proud of our flag.

It stands for our whole nation.

The bald eagle is on the U.S. seal.

It is our national bird.

The olive branch shows peace.

The arrows stand for strength.

The Statue of Liberty is a symbol.

It is in New York City.

She welcomes new visitors.

Her torch stands for freedom.

This is the Liberty Bell.

It is as old as our country.

It stands for freedom.

People visit it each year.

This is Mount Rushmore.

It shows four presidents.

They were great leaders who

helped shape our country.

How Do People Live Around the World?

People live in
different places.
How do they live?

My Words

language

law

Geography

1. People Talk to Each Other

All over the world, people talk.

They greet each other.

They say "hello" when they meet.

They say "bye" as they leave.

But people do not all speak
the same **language**.
They may say "nǐ haǒ" for "hello."
Or say "adios" for "bye."

2. Children Learn

Children in all places learn.

They learn to read and write.

They study math and science.

They may learn new languages.

But schools are not all the same.

Some meet on Saturday.

Classes can be big or small.

Students may dress the same.

3. People Eat Together

Many families eat together.

But meals may be different.

Some people eat with a fork.

Others eat with chopsticks.

4. Children Play

All children love to play.

Games may be the same, or not.

Hopscotch here may look

different in other places.

5. People Like Music

All people listen to music.

But the music may be different.

People can hear panpipes in Peru or bagpipes in Scotland.

6. People Follow Laws

Countries have **laws,** or rules.

Laws are different in each place.

People drive on the right here.

In England, they drive on the left.

Geography

Birthdays Then and Now

My birthday is soon.

Nana helps me plan my party.

Nana was once my age.

What was her birthday like?

We email my invitations.

They get there right away.

Nana's mom mailed hers.

They took two days to get there.

We will get a funny clown.

The Internet helps us find one.

Nana used a phone book.

She had to call places.

I look at cakes.

We take a picture with a phone.

When Nana was my age,

there were no cell phones.

We download songs.

We will play them at my party.

Nana played songs, too.

She used a record player.

I will blow out my candles.

Nana will take a video.

Nana has photos of her party.

They are black and white.

I pick out a new shirt.

I will wear it to my party.

Nana's mom made her a dress.

It had a white collar.

Lesson 9

It is easier to plan a party now.

Nana says, "A birthday party is

fun no matter when!"

I think so, too.

What Do People Need and Want?

All people have needs. They meet their needs in different ways.

My Words

needs

shelter

wants

Economics

1. We Have Needs

All around the world,

people have **needs**.

A need is something

people must have to live.

2. We Need Food

People in all places need food.

They get food in different ways.

Some buy fruits and vegetables.

Some grow food on a farm.

3. We Need Clothing

People all over the world

need clothes to wear.

In cold places, they wear coats.

In warm places, they wear shorts.

4. We Need Shelter

All people need **shelter**.

Some people buy a house.

Or they rent a place to live.

Some build their own home.

5. We Have Wants

People in all places
have different **wants**.

A want is something people
like but do not need.

6. We Want Different Things

Some children want a book.

Others want new markers.

We cannot get all of our wants.

What do you want?

I Make Choices When I Shop

My dad and I are running errands.

First, we make a to-do list.

Then we look at how much money

we can spend today.

First on the list is a haircut.

We go to a salon in the mall.

A woman cuts my hair.

Then my dad pays her.

Next we go to a clothing store.

I need a shirt for summer.

I find two shirts I want.

Can I get both of them?

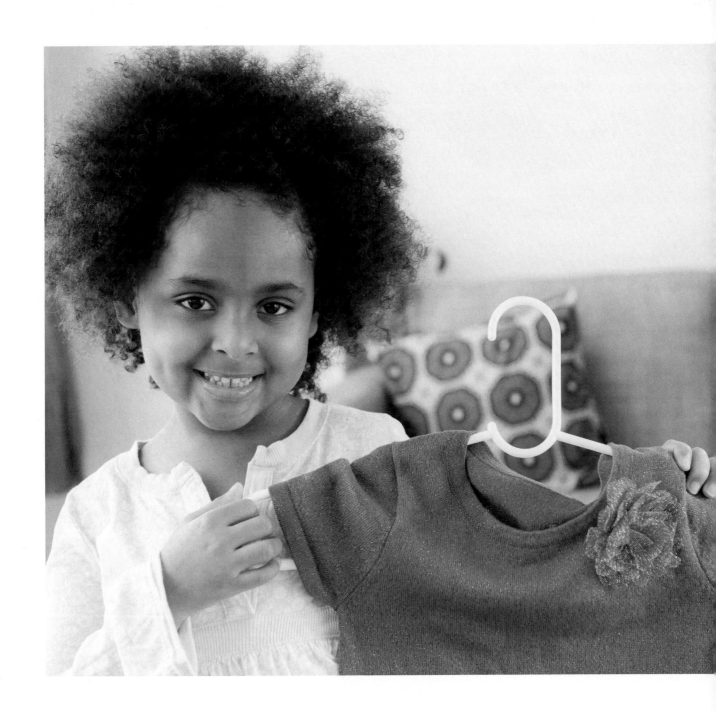

We look at the prices.

I cannot get both shirts.

I must choose only one.

We buy the one I like best.

How Can I Help Take Care of the World?

We all live on Earth.

We need to care for it.

How can I help?

My Words

garbage

recycle

reduce

reuse

Geography

1. Less Garbage

All people throw away **garbage**.

There is so much waste!

It can harm the land.

I should try to make less.

2. Recycling

I can **recycle** plastic and glass.

I can recycle cans and paper.

They become new things.

A bottle can turn into a jar.

3. Reusing

I can **reuse** my things.

An old sock is now a puppet.

My dad reuses an old tire.

The tire is now my swing.

4. Reducing

I can **reduce** my trash.

I can throw away less.

I use the same lunch box.

My mom reuses my containers.

Saving Money

I want to buy my dad a book.

His birthday is soon.

I will earn and save money.

Where will I keep my money?

My dad keeps money in a bank.

His money is safe there.

I will reuse an empty jar

and keep my money in it.

How can I earn money?

I can do extra chores.

I can rake leaves in the yard,

and my parents will pay me.

Do I have enough money?

I count it, but it's not enough.

I can do other jobs.

I can help wash the car.

Do I have enough money?

I count it, but I still need more.

I can sell lemonade.

Now, I have enough money!

I go to the used bookstore.

I hand the cashier my money.

I wrap the book in fancy paper.

"Happy birthday, Dad!"

I Can Learn About My World

Who is in my

neighborhood?

There are many families.

Each shares a past.

They live in our country.

 Civics   Geography History

My Family

How Can I Learn My Family's History?

My family shares a past.

I can ask questions.

I talk to my grandma.

She tells me stories from long ago.

We look at things from the past.

She shows me old photos.

They are black and white.

Life was different then.

Where Did My Family Come From?

I can look at a globe.

I find our home in the United States.

I find the place my family is from.

What is life like there?

Life is different in some ways.

We may not eat the same food.

Life is alike in some ways.

Families eat meals together.

What Does a Family Tree Show?

I can make a family tree.

I write the names of my relatives.

I draw a tree with my name on it.

I put the other names in the branches.

I share what I have learned.

I show my parents my family tree.

I draw a picture of my family and

tell them about our past.

My Neighborhood

Where Can I Learn in My Neighborhood?

What is my town's history?

I go to the library.

I ask the librarian for help.

He shows me books about my town.

What is there to do

in my neighborhood?

I go to the community center.

I sign up for an art class.

What should I do

if I feel sick or am hurt?

There is a doctor's office.

I go there to find out.

Nearby is the town hall.

There, people talk about our town.

They ask questions

and talk about town rules.

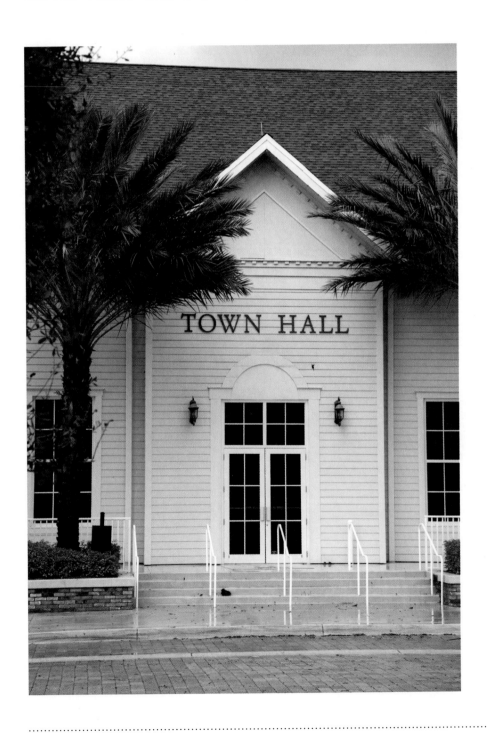

How Can I Show My Neighborhood?

I can make a map

of my neighborhood.

First, I draw the streets.

I use map symbols, too.

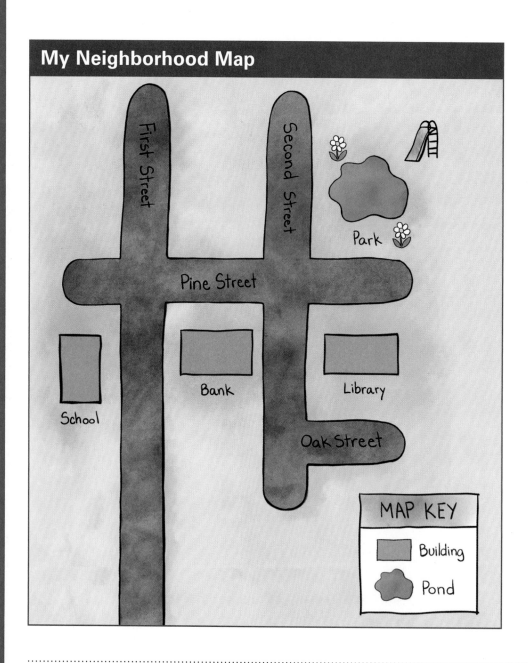

My Neighborhood Map

First Street

Second Street

Park

Pine Street

School

Bank

Library

Oak Street

MAP KEY

Building

Pond

I draw my house first.

Down the street is a mall.

Behind it is a bank.

What else is on my map?

My Country

How Do We Choose Leaders?

Our country has leaders.

Good leaders listen to others.

They help solve problems.

They make laws, too.

The Pledge of Allegiance

I pledge allegiance to the flag, of the United States of America and to the republic for which it stands, one nation under God, indivisible, with liberty and justice for all.

How Do I Show Pride in My Country?

I say the Pledge of Allegiance.

First, I put my hand on my heart.

I look at our country's flag.

Then we say the words together.

United States Map

Washington

Oregon

Montana

North
Dakota

South
Dakota

Idaho

Wyoming

Nebraska

Nevada

Utah

Colorado

California

Kansas

Arizona

New Mexico

*PACIFIC
OCEAN*

Texas

ARCTIC OCEAN

Alaska

*PACIFIC
OCEAN*

Hawaii

PACIFIC OCEAN

Minnesota

Wisconsin

Michigan

Iowa

Illinois

Indiana

Ohio

Missouri

Kentucky

West
Virginia

Virginia

New
York

Pennsylvania

New Hampshire

Vermont

Maine

Massachusetts

Rhode
Island

Connecticut

New Jersey

Delaware

Maryland

Washington
D.C.

North
Carolina

Tennessee

Oklahoma

Arkansas

South
Carolina

Mississippi

Alabama

Georgia

Louisiana

Florida

ATLANTIC
OCEAN

Gulf of Mexico

N
W   E
S

MAP KEY

⊛ U.S. capital

World Map

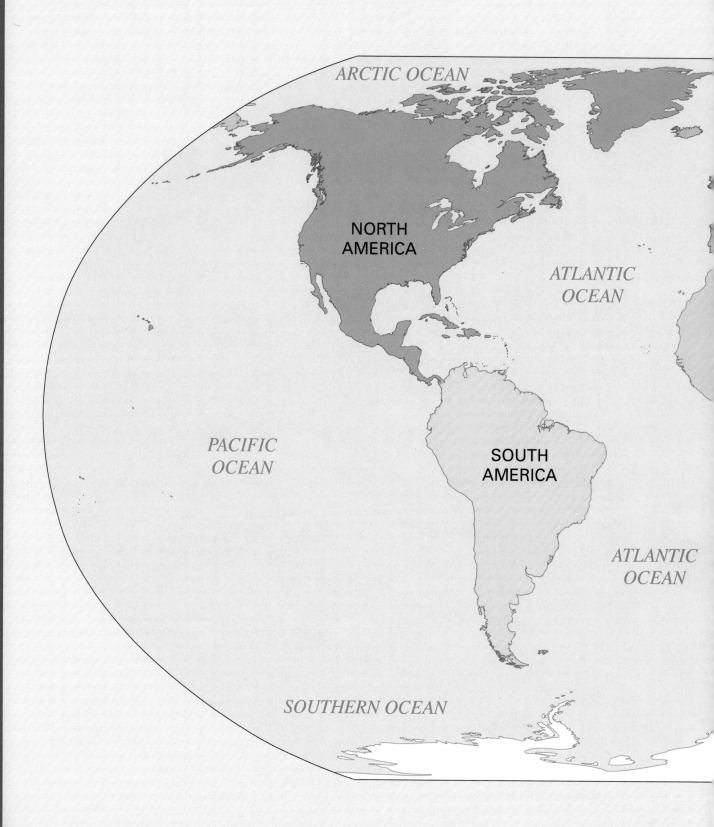

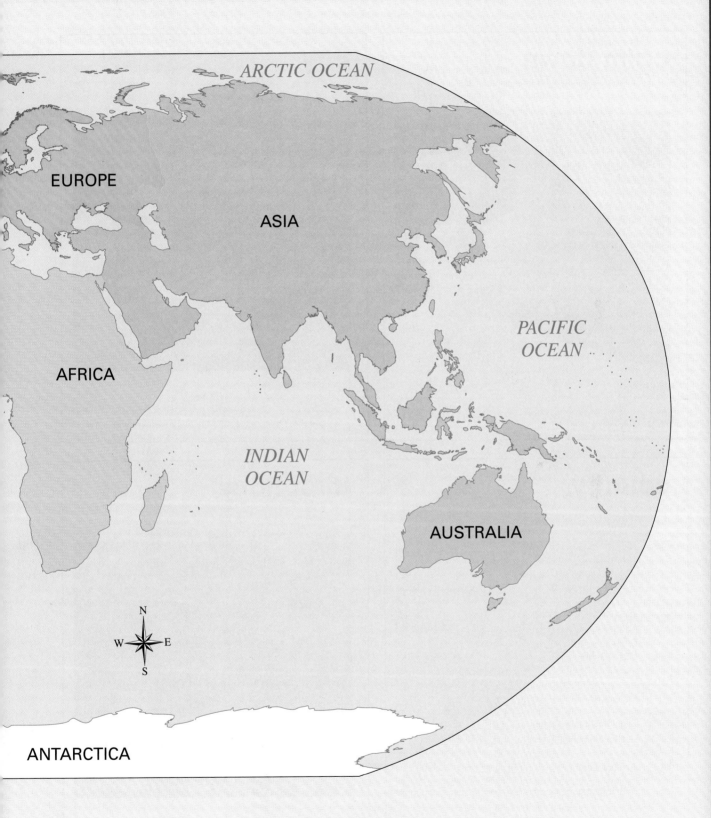

ARCTIC OCEAN

EUROPE

ASIA

PACIFIC
OCEAN

AFRICA

INDIAN
OCEAN

AUSTRALIA

ANTARCTICA

calm down

city

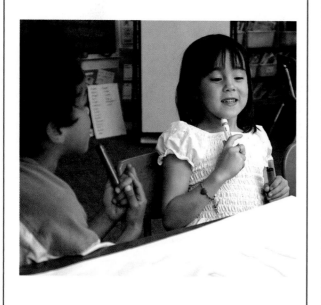

country

directions

family

feelings

garbage

get along

introduce

language

law

map

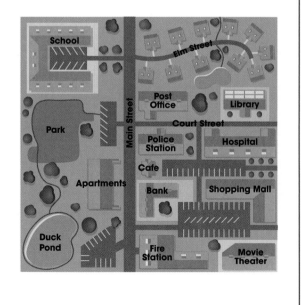

needs

neighbor

neighborhood

problem

recycle

reduce

reuse

shelter

solve

special

state

Idaho

Nevada

Utah

California

Arizona

PACIFIC
OCEAN

tradition

vote

wants

world

Cover and Title Page
Cover: Getty Images

Front Matter
i: Thinkstock **vi L:** Ariel Skelley/Blend Images/Corbis **vi R:** Ariel Skelley/Blend Images/Corbis **vii:** Thinkstock **viii:** Thinkstock **viii:** Thinkstock **ix:** Thinkstock **ix:** Thinkstock **xii:** Thinkstock **xii:** Thinkstock **xii:** Thinkstock **xiii:** Shutterstock **xiii:** Thinkstock **xiii:** Cultura Creative (RF)/Alamy **xiv:** iStockphoto **xiv:** iStockphoto **xiv:** Yan Liao/Alamy **xv:** Dmitry Kalinovsky/Dreamstime **xv:** iStockphoto **xvi:** Shutterstock **1:** Library of Congress

Lesson 1
2: Thinkstock **4:** iStockphoto **5:** Thinkstock **7:** Petro/Dreamstime **8:** MPVHistory/Alamy **9:** MPVHistory/Alamy **10:** iStockphoto **11:** Getty Images

Lesson 2
12: Thinkstock **14:** Thinkstock **15:** Thinkstock **16:** iStockphoto **17 TL:** Thinkstock **17 BL:** Thinkstock **17 R:** Thinkstock **18:** Thinkstock/SuperStock **19 L:** Thinkstock **19 R:** Copyright Redlink/Corbis/AP Images **20:** Thinkstock **21:** iStockphoto **23:** iStockphoto **24:** Enigma/Alamy **25:** The Granger Collection, NY **26:** Stocktrek Images, Inc./Alamy **27:** Library of Congress **28:** Thomas Lozinski/Dreamstime **29:** iStockphoto

Lesson 3
30: Thinkstock **32:** Thinkstock **33:** Goldenkb/Dreamstime **34:** Thinkstock **36:** Shutterstock **37:** Blend Images/Alamy **38:** iStockphoto **39:** Shutterstock **40:** Dennis MacDonald/Alamy **41:** Laurence Mouton/PhotoAlto/Corbis

Lesson 4
42: Shutterstock **44:** Androniques/Dreamstime **45:** Tom Grill/Corbis **47:** iStockphoto **48:** Thinkstock **49:** North Wind Picture Archives/Alamy **50:** The Granger Collection, NY **51:** Thinkstock **52:** GL Archive/Alamy **53:** MBI/Alamy

Lesson 5
54: Thinkstock **60 L:** Ariel Skelley/Blend Images/Corbis **60 R:** Ariel Skelley/Blend Images/Corbis **61:** Thinkstock **62:** Thinkstock **63:** Getty Images **64:** Thinkstock **65:** Thinkstock **66:** Erik Isakson/Tetra Images/Corbis **67:** Erik Isakson/Tetra Images/Corbis

Lesson 6
68: Cultura Creative (RF)/Alamy **70:** iStockphoto **71 L:** iStockphoto **71 R:** iStockphoto **72:** iStockphoto **73:** iStockphoto **74:** Blend Images/Superstock **75 R:** iStockphoto **76 L:** Fancy Collection/Superstock **77 R:** Thinkstock **78 L:** David Buffington/Exactostock-1598/Superstock **79 L:** XiXinXing/Superstock **80 L:** Thinkstock **81 R:** iStockphoto

Lesson 7
82: iStockphoto **84 L:** Thinkstock **84 R:** Thinkstock **85 T:** iStockphoto **85 B:** Ellen Isaacs/Alamy **86 TL:** Thinkstock **86 R:** Thinkstock **86 BL:** MBI/Alamy **87 T:** Thinkstock **87 BL:** iStockphoto **87 BR:** iStockphoto **88:** Seamartini/Dreamstime **90 L:** Golden Pixels LLC/Alamy **90 R:** Barry Diomede/Alamy **91:** John Steel/Alamy **92:** Library of Congress **93:** Library of Congress **94:** Library of Congress **95:** Library of Congress **96:** Library of Congress **97:** Mary Altaffer/AP/Corbis **98 L:** Library of Congress **98 R:** Thinkstock **99 T:** Golden Pixels LLC/Alamy **99 B:** Purestock/Alamy

Lesson 8
100: iStockphoto **102:** iStockphoto **103 L:** Thinkstock **103 R:** Viktor Pravdica/Dreamstime **104 TL:** Elultimodeseo/Dreamstime **104 TR:** iStockphoto **104 BL:** iStockphoto **104 BR:** iStockphoto **105:** Thinkstock **107:** NASA/Corbis **108 TL:** Shutterstock **108 TR:** Thinkstock **108 BL:** Juergen Priewe/Dreamstime **108 BR:** Thinkstock **109:** Mrcmos/Dreamstime **110:** Zoonar GmbH/Alamy **111 L:** Image Source/Getty Images **111 R:** Lydie Desriac/Dreamstime **112:** Michael Ventura/Alamy **113:** James Randklev/Photographer's Choice RF/Getty Images